The Convex Mirror

Collected Poems

OTHER BOOKS BY SAMUEL YELLEN

New and Selected Poems
In the House and Out, and Other Poems
The Passionate Shepherd: A Book of Stories
The Wedding Band (a novel)
American Labor Struggles

The Convex Mirror

Collected Poems

Samuel Yellen

Indiana University Press

Bloomington · London

Published in Canada by Fitzhenry & Whiteside Limited,
Don Mills, Ontario
Library of Congress catalog card number: 72–135016
ISBN: 253-11340-7

MANUFACTURED IN THE UNITED STATES OF AMERICA

In the House and Out, and Other Poems, copyright 1952 by Samuel Yellen. *New and Selected
Poems*, copyright 1964 by the Indiana University Press.

The poems *Here in This Garden, Epitaph for a Committee* (1943), *Today's Horoscope* (1945),
Indian Summer (1946), *Samuel Pepys and the Dutch Lass, Wanted, This August Sun* (1947),
First Grade, Room 1, South Case School; Read This Face (1948), *Song Without Black Notes,
Personal* (1951), and *The Convex Mirror* (1952) were copyrighted, in the respective years
shown, by The New Yorker Magazine, Inc.

The poems *Signs of the Times, They Say the Last Supper Is Badly Damaged, As I Was Walk-
ing Down Fifth Avenue, The Colony, East Wind, Grisaille with a Spot of Red, The Dream,*
copyrighted in 1949, 1951, 1953, 1954, 1957 by The Antioch Review.

Poems © 1945, 1952, 1953, 1954, 1956 by The New York Times Company. Reprinted by per-
mission.

Auto Trip reprinted by permission from the May, 1954, issue of Good Housekeeping Maga-
zine. © 1954 by the Hearst Corporation. *Lullaby* reprinted by permission from the September,
1951, issue of Good Housekeeping Magazine. © 1951 by the Hearst Corporation.

Autumn Forecast and *Gnarled Oak*, courtesy, Washington (D.C.) Star.

Little Exercise in Pessimism, copyright © 1955, by the Atlantic Monthly Company, Boston,
Mass. Reprinted with permission.

To Edna

I should bring to you as love token
Not a book of words, not poetry
Which is all contrivance and artifice,
But a piece of driftwood thrown up by the sea,
A sand dollar, a pebble, a periwinkle shell,
A blue jay's feather, an apple, an oak leaf,
A branch of flowering quince, a gourd,
Some ears of corn bound in a harvest sheaf.

For you yourself are without artifice,
Like a skip-and-a-jump or a country-dance;
You shed your graces on the here and now,
And give each moment its resonance.
You read by smile, by sigh, by tear,
By drift of cloud, by song of bird;
And you listen for what sounds behind
The always always ambiguous word.

When a child brings you his work of art,
You never ask which is house, which is train,
Why the cow is green, the man purple,
Why an eleven-sided windowpane:
You simply take his gift as simple gift.
And so, in return for love and renewed life,
Take this book which I give to you,
My good friend, my beloved, my wife.

Acknowledgments

Many of the poems in this collection first appeared in periodicals. For permission to reprint, I express my thanks to the editors of the *American Mercury, American Scholar, Antioch Review, Atlantic Monthly, Christian Science Monitor, Commentary, Commonweal, Folio, Forum, Good Housekeeping, Menorah Journal, Nation, New Mexico Quarterly, New Poems by American Poets #1* and *#2* (Ballantine), *New Yorker, New York Herald Tribune, New York Times, Pacific Spectator, Providence Sunday Journal, Saturday Evening Post, Southwest Review, Tomorrow, University of Kansas City Review, Washington Evening Star,* and *Yale Review.*

Contents

The Convex Mirror

Collected Poems

The Convex Mirror

Avenues of shimmer lead into the bellied mirror
Above the manteltree; and while we may not enter,
Off in that remote magnetic center
Each of us has a minikin ambassador.

There where right is left and left is right,
Floor curls into ceiling, objects warp and yaw,
And business is conducted in a Mardi gras
Amid a whirlabout of colored carnival lights.

Of course, no sound can penetrate to our senses;
And yet we almost hear tinkling glockenspiel,
Steam calliope, whistles, tootles, bells,
And fiddles fiddling gay Hungarian dances.

I cannot hold back, the revelry is *there*.
As heart in hand I eagerly approach,
I see a droll homunculus detach
Himself and skip toward me with many a leer.

That advancing figure could not be absurder:
Where I am thin and trim he is fat and blown,
His legs are crooked, his head is not quite on,
He puffs his face against his homeland's border.

We almost touch—almost—not quite, not quite!
The fault is mine: *I* am the faint withholder.
The trouble is *my* head is on my shoulders,
The trouble is *my* head is screwed on tight.

First Grade, Room 1, South Case School

There I stand, second row, fourth from the right,
Arms rigid at my sides, obedient,
A scholar, though perhaps not erudite,
My eyes upon the camera eye intent.

Rebuke or guile has forced each banal pose.
One wears the hackneyed toothless grin, and one
Out of brand-new shoes, like a flower, grows.
One girl sits scowling, a wee Amazon.

All the trappings of innocence are here:
Curls and ribbons, stockings hanging in rolls,
Starched dress, sailor suit, protruding ear.
But who would say that these are simple souls?

One is perplexed, contempt curls another's lip,
One has known terror, one has learned aplomb,
One smirks in fraudulent good-fellowship,
One is withdrawn in philosophic calm.

But I, or rather he who bore my name—
He surveys me with enigmatic face.
Likeness there is, yet we are not the same;
For he stands there, and I am in this place.

That stranger in the prim wide-collared blouse
Is, so Wordsworth said, Father of the Man.
I tell you from my shaded prison-house,
Out of that ugly duckling came no swan.

Why have I no keepsake of one small heart
Beating out the minutes of that lost day?
Whence came these trackless seas to hold apart
The Man here and that forlorn castaway?

Little Father, there is no turning back;
I go my journey at a grim command.
But you I carry in my haversack;
Together we go on, though not hand in hand.

The Snail

The snail is the perfect solipsist:
For home, secretes his spiral past,
And since he likes the dark and damp,
Dwells inside without a lamp.

There the I is never free
Of its autobiography;
Comes outside his armor-plate
Only to feed and copulate.

At times puts forth his horns and snout,
And then discreetly looks about;
But in a moment will withdraw
To misinterpret what he saw.

Lives as furtive as an elf,
Broods and dreams, cuckolds himself:
And from the slime left by the snail,
The sun contrives a silver trail.

A Time of Light, a Time of Shadow

School was out. The boys were quelling Mars with death-ray gun,
The girls were going to Heaven via hopscotch,
One little toddler and one dog presumed to join the fun,
And in a scientific mood I paused to watch.

The sunlight fell about them in a cataract:
If there was shadow, then the very shadow shone;
If there was substance, that substance did not reflect
The light, but let it pass through flesh and bone.

Not yet cemented by one central will,
Each childish body simply flew apart;
Legs and arms cascaded in a random spill,
And shadows had to find their way by fit and start.

It was a time of light. Disembodied ripple,
Incorporeal speed and movement thrilled the air;
A fabric without density, a purest dapple
Would leap away and leave its shadow there.

Detached, disjoined, having lost their accustomed tether,
Those shadows twitched and fluttered in bewilderment:
They needed something, if no more than a feather,
Yet had no notion where that something went.

And watching those spirits, like luminous buttercups,
Fly by and throw no darkness as they passed,
I too presumed, and tried three small self-conscious hops;
But my shadow dragged along, mine I could not cast.

And then I saw how shadow bides its time,
How the brightest transparencies will turn opaque,
Sheer speed and animation will go lame,
And heavy shadow pile up flake by flake.

The Wooden Tiger

This tiger is not Blake's tiger burning bright:
Some *mortal* hand framed this fearful symmetry,
Hewed and whittled out of wood this life-size counterfeit.
And wood is not a bad kind of flesh, being free
Of rapid depreciation by animal chemistry.

The model was no domesticated pussycat,
But the real thing in total recall down to vibrant tail.
The cunning hand made use of woody grain, whorl, knot,
To hint at muscle, rib, and haunch-bone, all carved to scale,
Eight savage feet from whiskered nose to tip of tail.

A century has not slackened the wide cruel grin;
And while some seams have given along the sides and back,
The undimmed colors still ring out—the rufous brown
To burn through green leaves, the white cheeks and belly,
    the black
Traverse stripes arching down and under from the back.

This is a dread man-eater. The evidence is clear.
The teeth are worn and defective, and one stump is gone.
But most conclusive, the hand that worked with loving care
Has been swallowed up, bequeathing us this cryptic yawn—
At least there is no doubt the mortal hand is gone.

Yes, the hand which forged the wood by oil or candlelight,
Bodying forth into view and thus putting out of mind
What burned and flickered there in the phosphorescent night,
Has long since disappeared, yet prankishly left behind
This beast denied forever the forests of the mind.

And now the wooden tiger, come far from its last kill,
Haunts our little clearing on the outskirts of the jungle,
No longer gratified by wild hog, deer, or peafowl.
If it would pounce and strike, we could trust it not to bungle;
But it prowls forever powerless, cut off from its jungle.

Beast Fable

I catch a minute by the tail and hold it fast. . . .
—WILLIAM COWPER, *Letter to the Reverend*
William Unwin, August 24, 1786

I catch a minute by the tail and hold it fast,
And as it turns to stare at me with fishy eye,
The gill arches pulse, the tapering body tugs and twists,
The spangles of saffron, bronze, rose, and lazuli
Shimmer beneath the iridescent ocean film.
My fingers clutch, lest the slippery prize be lost
In the abyss whence it so miraculously came.

Enameled scales dissolve to sleek black panther side:
Within the furry black I trace each black rosette,
And press my cheek until my hot pounding blood
Couples with the blood of that voluptuous cheat.
A laugh but once removed from *vox humana*
Jerks me loose from suddenly foul bristle-coat,
To goggle at grinning chops of striped hyena.

And still I hold fast as turquoise-bottomed baboon
Mocks my fine solemnities with monkey antics;
But just when I foolishly relent and turn buffoon,
I find myself in subterranean labyrinthics,
Dragged through narrow passageways by a blind old mole
Under crumbling heavens—for faint stars and moon,
Phosphorescent roots of liverwort and toadstool.

Mole glitters now as ruby-throated hummmingbird,
Dizzily I ride while through the bright air it flashes;
Far below, town, street, field, and river, all grow blurred,
Till beating wings catch fire and fall to earth in ashes.
A glaucous raucous parrot steps forth from the last flicker,
Shakes its painted plumage, and cries as hooked bill slashes:
"Polly wants a cracker, wants a cracker, wants a cracker."
Feathers fuse, and thick-plated rhinoceros careers

Through the swart jungle, swinging me by its caudal stump;
Bangs flanks against splintered trees, savagely jars
The ground, thunders, crashes, plunges into a swamp.
Then out of the mud yawns a crenelated smile:
I take due notice of the hypocritic tears,
And tumble down the gullet of the crocodile.

Pygmalion and Galatea

And thus they come upon the Winter of their lives.
Her eye, gem-like, carved with a sharp-edged tool,
Perceives too readily the clown, the dupe, the fool;
No matter with what cunning he contrives,
Caught in the hard relentless glare
He is stripped bare.

The leaves have fallen. There is no turning back.
Past the rubble and crumbling statues of that place
He stumbles on. A smile puckers his face.
His eye, but a blob of jelly in a filmy sac,
Finds her in charitable shadow, as at night
By candlelight.

Where others see the cross and whiskered hag,
He sees a princess of ineffable charm;
His hand caresses a firm ivory-smooth arm,
Where other fingers trace the wrinkle snag.
For him alone is her throat philomel
Casting a spell.

A stately queen, she entertains his homage,
Accepts his abject worship as her proper due.
The image in his heart, how other than bright and true?
For she too has fashioned of herself an image,
And the image she carries in her heart is
Even lovelier than his.

The Lesson

Papa was teaching him to tell time:
What he was to tell time he didn't understand.
But he knew that if he learned he would have a dime,
And he frowned avidly on hour-hand and minute-hand.

He was still little enough boy to sit on Papa's lap;
Nearby on the table stood the ticking clock.
But where was time? Would the numbers on the dial clap
Hands and show him? Or the steady tick-and-tock and tick-and-tock?

He knew time to wake up and time to go to bed:
But he hadn't had time to learn time you waste and time you kill,
Time is limited and time is unlimited,
Time runs uphill and time runs downhill,

Time on your hands and no time to wait,
Time there is, time there isn't, and time foreclosed,
Time is character, time is fate,
And time is when time leaves you mortally exposed.

At that time he had no time for why, or what, or how;
His time was taken up with who and when:
Time was the Mouse Ran up the Clock, the Cow
Jumped over the Moon, the Little Red Hen.

But as he was learning to tell before and after,
And either made a mistake or was at his cleverest,
Why suddenly amid all the merry laughter
Did Papa sob and hug him to his breast?

Lullaby for Joanna

Lay down your golden hairpin,
Take off your silver slipper;
It's time to get you ready
To ride the Little Dipper.

Unclasp your coral girdle,
Brush your silken hair;
It's time to take your place
In Cassiopeia's Chair.

Slip into your nightgown,
Lie down straight and narrow;
It's time to hunt the Dragon,
It's time to shoot the Arrow.

Call forth a jeweled dream,
Kiss the moon goodnight,
Close your pearl eyelids;
Sleep tight, my dear, sleep tight.

Song Without Black Notes

Fa una canzone senza note nere.
—*Canzonetta* by Orazio Vecchi
(1550–1603)

Take hazel for eyes, amber for hair,
Coral for tip of pointed ear,
Ivory for wrist and throat,
And make a song without black notes.

Take violet for love's unreason,
Green for cunning, orange for treason,
White for flicker of petticoat,
And make a song without black notes.

Take azure serpent with blue-green head,
Timorous doe pale red, pale red,
Tipsy bearded saffron goat,
And make a song without black notes.

Samuel Pepys
and the Dutch Lass

*Back by water, where a pretty,
sober, Dutch lass sat reading all
the way, and I could not fasten
any discourse upon her.*
        —*Diary*, May 18, 1660

She was pretty,
But she was sober;
In body, May;
In mien, October.

She brought a flutter
To his heart;
He set to work
With all his art.

But his discourse
Would not fasten;
It fell before
A cold assassin.

No response,
No smile, no look;
She kept her eyes
Upon her book.

Raconteur: Age Three

You tell me a terrible story,
And while the syntax is tangled,
I judge the details are gory
And more than grammar lies mangled.

Though present is snarled with past,
Fact confounded with wish,
I gather the action is fast
And likely to chill the flesh.

Your tongue is a galloping steed,
You ride it boldly astraddle:
Caution does not cut the speed,
Prudence is not in the saddle.

But the gallop will slow to a trot;
The steed, reined in by guile,
Will learn when to canter, when not,
And walk a crooked mile.

Wanted

Goes by the name of Bob or Harry,
Charlie, Jim, or Bill;
Last reported seen in Scranton,
Dallas, and Evansville.

Tends to fat around the waist,
No visible mark or scar;
Doesn't mind if he has a drink—
His manner is jocular.

Is fond of children, partial to women,
Likes to flash a wad;
Prefers traveling alone.—Wanted
For use of the mails to defraud.

Wrote a letter to his sweetheart,
Called her Toots and Hon;
Failed to mention a little number,
Called her his Only One.

Wrote a letter to his friend,
Hoped to see him soon;
Praised him to his face, but elsewhere
Sang a different tune.

Sent a postcard to his brother,
Said he wished him well;
The thorn festering in his heart—
That he would not tell.

Beware! This man is dangerous,
Quick to cheat and connive.
Reward for information leading
To his capture—dead or alive.

Personal

Cultured gentleman, mature, congenial, refined,
Philosophical background, idealistic by nature,
Fond of music, sense of humor, scintillating mind,
Introspective, shy, shy as some small forest creature,
Invites exchange of views with feminine counterpart,
Discerning, amiable, unselfish young lady who shares
His deep interests and, in communing with a lonely heart,
Will not be frightened off by a few gray hairs.

Middle-aged woman, personable, gracious, loving fun and life,
Sophisticated, independent, with unslaked curiosity,
Partial to the pursuit of happiness, having had enough
Of convention and Lenten fare, unencumbered, fancy-free,
Seeks adventure via correspondence,
Easement, margin where time now cramps and pinches,
Diversion, experience, warmth, abundance
Where life has denied, sitting on its thin haunches.

Solitary young introvert, disillusioned, cynical,
Educated beyond endurance, bored, bored, bored,
Versatile, intelligent, creative, highly original,
Hopeful of striking responsive chord,
Desires letters from fellow iconoclast,
Seeks escape from tedium's dominion,
Invites the piquant, the provocative, the unexpressed,
Desires—*Arcades ambo*—a lost soul's companion.

Invites, seeks, desires—the sleazy words stick in the craw!
Where are the desperate words, the words to compel and enjoin?
Alas, those victims of a kind of Gresham's law
Have been driven into hiding by this debased coin.
Seeks, invites, desires! Will these words penetrate,
Touch, arouse? Oh, will someone hear
Before *Too late, Too late, Too late, Too late*
Becomes a deafening clamor in the ear?

17

How I Found Truth

As I drew near,
Truth was a rock,
But shimmering air
Played many a trick.

Water came over,
Light was bent:
All grew waver,
Buckle, and tint.

The rock was hung
With fantastic lace,
Pulsing things clung
To kelp and moss.

The worldly scene
In that foliage
Turned Byzantine,
And I a doge.

My rich crown nodded,
The image approached,
Yet sank and faded
When I reached.

There fern, shell, and rose
Bloomed and thrived:
My strange head ablaze,
Down I dived.

Bone and cartilage
Snapped apart,
And the rock's knife-edge
Entered my heart.

Nighthawks

After the painting by Edward Hopper

The place is the corner of Empty and Bleak,
The time is night's most desolate hour,
The scene is Al's Coffee Cup or the Hamburger Tower,
The persons in this drama do not speak.

We who peer through that curve of plate glass
Count three nighthawks seated there—patrons of life:
The counterman will be with you in a jiff,
The thick white mugs were never meant for demitasse.

The single man whose hunched back we see
Once put a gun to his head in Russian roulette,
Whirled the chamber, pulled the trigger, won the bet,
And now lives out his x years' guarantee.

And facing us, the two central characters
Have finished their coffee, and have lit
A contemplative cigarette;
His hand lies close, but not touching hers.

Not long ago together in a darkened room,
Mouth burned mouth, flesh beat and ground
On ravaged flesh, and yet they found
No local habitation and no name.

Oh, are we not lucky to be none of these!
We can look on with complacent eye:
Our satisfactions satisfy,
Our pleasures, our pleasures please.

The Children's Hour

Who can tell what the moment will make of them?
Out of their repertoire, what fantastic role,
With merely a cry to confirm the swift and sudden
Transmigration of the soul?

The air throbs with shrill incantations;
One word turns beggars into princes and billionaires,
Another stamps contours on the shapeless future.
Whatever the whim, the word, the all-powerful word is theirs.

Here is a world where syntax and logic are unborn,
Things hold together without glue or nails.
The living die easily showing no surprise;
Quickly they rise again. These dead men tell tales.

This hour lies free of the bonds of time.
This prologue makes trial of what the years will bring;
But here is no ruthless game of forfeits,
Here are stations of the cross without the suffering.

Nothing is what it is. Objects are but stage properties.
Persons in the play are here today and gone tomorrow.
Pang and spasm do not erode this mortal tissue,
This lamentation is but the forgery of sorrow.

These players have not met Abiding Consequence,
Nor have they seen the Specter of Probability.
The closing down of night holds no shaking terror,
And sleep wipes clean the tablets of their memory.

The Mourning Dove

In a low branch I saw a mourning dove
Sitting motionless upon a flimsy nest
Of twigs and leaf stems loose-woven, uncemented:
The bird had turned to alabaster subtly tinted,
But could not still the ticking in its breast.

And then one day two ragged ruffled fledglings
Peeped from underneath that polished elegance.
The bird mother perched there, the small reptilian head
Fixed, immovable, each eye a topaz bead
That watched and did not waver from my glance.

In the night a wind arose. The next morning found
The nest blown down, a mere unraveled litter,
Twig and leaf stem scattered across the ground.
Something had been at it: the jewel glitter
Of excrement was there, but the fledglings were gone.

The bird mother roosted where the nest had been,
With only those heartbeats to tick the time:
Whether it was Instinct, or some Master Plan,
Or simply a body itch as yet unsatisfied,
The bird had frozen in mournful pantomime.

I gazed at that rare shape and each painted spot;
While, dupe of instinct, victim of itch, or emblem of grief,
The dove gazed back, an object carved.
We gazed and gazed, till I forgot
Which was observer, and which observed.

The Nativity

The first days of Winter bend the wind to the north,
A fractured stalk of corn rattles in its socket.
Beneath, where my leg bones jar on the frozen earth,
Each mole and hedgehog lies curled up in a pocket.

Night falls. One last leaf clatters against a bough.
Sentence has been passed, there can be no acquittal.
At my feet the dead leaves scratch and scrape. Now,
Things that once were soft are become hard and brittle.

Off in the distance a dog incessantly barks.
The Archer climbs clear above the south horizon:
His hoofs on the metallic blue stamp out cold sparks,
Arrows of stinging sleet announce his season.

Transfigured water hangs in spikes and nails
From the window sill. Senses grow numb, fingers stiffen,
Ice flourishes. A bush puts on scales
And before my eyes turns to quaint winged griffin.

I press my face against the windowpane
Through the frost flowers that bloom there in the night,
And though my body waits outside I look in
Upon the tinsel figures and lozenges of light.

Like a jigsaw puzzle slightly jogged apart,
The shepherds, each richly crowned with a sea anemone,
Stand around the manger, hats crumpled to the heart,
And gaze down transfixed upon the bright Nativity.

Concrete Poem

```
OOOOOOOOOOOOOOOOOOOO
OOOOOOOOOOOOOOOOOOOO
OOOOOOOO there OOOOOOOO
OOOOOOOOOOOOOOOOOOOO
OOOOOOOOO is OOOOOOOOO
OOOOOOOOOOOOOOOOOOOO
OOOOOOOO less OOOOOOOO
OOOOOOOOOOOOOOOOOOOO
OOOOOOOO here OOOOOOOO
OOOOOOOOOOOOOOOOOOOO
OOOOOOOO than OOOOOOOO
OOOOOOOOOOOOOOOOOOOO
OOOOOOO meets OOOOOOO
OOOOOOOOOOOOOOOOOOOO
OOOOOOOO the OOOOOOOO
OOOOOOOOOOOOOOOOOOOO
OOOOOOOO eye OOOOOOOO
OOOOOOOOOOOOOOOOOOOO
OOOOOOOOOOOOOOOOOOOO
```

The Colony

The colony numbered some scores of souls,
All manner of men, even a woman and a child or two,
Some with hands and feet, some with claws, hoofs, jowls,
Moving by fits and starts, making a hullabaloo:
Hypocrite, sneak, liar, coward, egotist,
Yes, and the lecher, the faker, the mischief-maker
Quarreled, embraced, scratched, kicked, and kissed.

Here, mincing his steps like a dancing master,
One balanced on outstretched hands a house of cards
Kept trembling just this side of disaster
By a broken wishbone and mumbo-jumbo words;
And there, a child ran laughing under the trees,
Not unaware of each engaging posture,
His laughter inflected by eagerness to please.

Above, one floated, reclining on a cloud
Antiquely tinted primrose, puce, and rubric,
With castles, ladies, unicorns in elusive thread
Woven through the frail and fickle fabric.
Below, one plodded, tolling grievous groans
Out of a shrunken head, and, for *memento mori*,
Clacking and rattling a chain of human bones.

Out on the road, one lurched in crooked circles,
With unhinged face contorted, about to blubber—
Wild fire shot from his eyes in sparkles,
His fist gripped a dagger of gray indiarubber;
While yet another trod on his very heel,
Now swelling, now dwindling like a shadow,
And clutched a jagged knife of bloodstained steel.

And three clowns staggered across the village green,
Gravely halting every now and then to salaam,
And a cowbell round the neck of him between
Clanked *Look, here I am! Look, here I am! Look, here I am!*
Accosting them, I asked: "How call you this colony?"
They stared at me as if *I* were the sleepwalker,
Then leered and said: " 'Tis yclept Imyselfandme."

The Cloisters

Fort Tryon Park—New York

Here in the Cloisters a fourth dimension evolves,
A remote time-place of monk, knight, and herald;
Here other men once made *their* peace with the world,
And that much harder peace, peace with themselves.

Today I walk alone in the silence almost heard,
The seven-century hush transported stone by stone
To this alien ground. I listen here alone,
The little fountain trills the clear song of a bird.

Though much here is "restored," much remains the same:
Carved angel, beast, placid and tormented soul
Gaze down from corbel, lintel, capital
Upon the same fevered flesh in frantic search of balm.

The cloister flowers, blue, gold, purple, pink, and white,
Are those once stained in glass, woven in tapestries—
Jonquils, hyacinths, daisies, violets, fleurs-de-lys,
The colors somewhat slack in this less brilliant light.

Through the western arches, as in painted fantasy,
Beyond the broad Hudson's rippling sheens and shades
Rise the riven rusts of the sculptured Palisades,
And there for perspective against the sky a gull soars free.

Oh, I, I am a cheerless captive the cloister stones embrace.
I touch one stone decayed, not by time nor rain,
But by ingesting sorrow, passion, guilt, and pain,
A stone worn soft and gentle as a human face.

The sour corrupting acids are sucked up from my breast.
Who gives me this stone gives me a healing herb
With infinite capacity to draw out and absorb:
A smile denotes the cheerless captive become the cheerful guest.

Easter Meditation

Bridal wreath now plies the loom
Until its green in white is drowned,
Bowing low with weight of bloom,
Spilling light along the ground.

Green and white are Easter hues,
Token of the empty tomb,
Bringing long-awaited news
Of present birth and coming doom.

The earth's great heartbeat makes no sound;
Yet we shall see this bright shrub lose
Bloom and leaf, and show ungowned
What we accept but do not choose.

Spring Song

The sky is blue, the clouds are soft,
The sunshine throbs with the twang of a harp,
The new-born green lights up the branch,
But the wind is sharp, the wind is sharp.

Primrose and violet raise their heads,
The crocus drips untainted gold,
You can hear the shoots stir last year's leaves,
But the wind is cold, the wind is cold.

The earth's tough hide relents and thaws,
But man, poor man, is thinner skinned;
Oh, sun, burn through the cosmic void,
Warm up the wind, warm up the wind.

Auto Trip

After the winding roads, the hills, mesas, ridges,
The restorations, monuments, historic mansions, old forts,
Canyons, waterfalls, rivers, covered and uncovered bridges,
The sweating red-faced men, their wives in halter and shorts:

After the lookout points and observations towers,
The fine vistas, distant glimpses, panoramas,
The quaint customs, panhandling bears, colorful flowers,
The small children lost and crying for their mammas:

After the gas stations, rest rooms, motels, starts late and early,
The relic of ancient times, the stopover, the side trip,
The souvenir stands, the landmarks, the waitresses smiling or surly,
The home of the onion, the peanut, the wooden match, the paper clip:

After the Romes, Londons, Amsterdams Old and New,
The Horns and Rocks and Falls both Big and Little,
The natural wonder, queen city, gateway, scenic view,
The dawns and sunsets and incessant fender rattle:

After all the blur and welter, what, what for keepsake?—
A solitary bird call heard across a breathing space,
A slant of sky fallen into a lake,
And gaunt gray death looking out of a stranger's face.

The Emmet

At my shoe tip lay a roadside jungle,
No less a wilderness for being small;
Knotgrass, thistle, and wild onion tangled
With vine and nettle in a prickly caul.
Beneath the snarled membrane all was shadow:
Tiger beetle lurked in screened crevasse
To pounce on victim crossing pigmy meadow,
And spider skulked behind a blade of grass.

Tinfoil and clinker threw a sickly luster,
Shard of glass looked out with wicked glare;
Under a moldy paper strange sights festered—
Spines, fungus growths, and plants with hair.
That was a world where broken tile and bottle,
Things that squirm and things that putrefy
Turned ruby, pearl, precious stone and metal,
Marvels of frenzied shape and savage dye.

All at once a frail two-legged emmet
Scuttled timorous upon the scene,
Came to a knob, clambered to its summit,
Scanned the round horizon, stopped to preen;
Then alert from toe to twitching feeler,
Thought it heard a noise and stood there tense;
Reassured, it stretched to show up taller,
Stared down with scorn from its eminence.

Lost in thought, it dreamed a dazzling peril,
Entered the labyrinth of a mad romance,
Smiled to see itself so brave and virile,
Executed a brief triumphal dance;
Then looked if there were witness to its folly,
Fancied the echo of a hooting gibe,
Found no one, felt a trifle silly,
And knew itself a member of its tribe.

And knowing, beheld its self-esteem unravel,
Sat there head in hands, ashamed, contrite,
Confusing what it feared to do with evil,
Quick to take alarm in the fading light.
I towered above, while that fragile creature,
But lately wriggled from its warm tight womb,
Cringing and toadying true to its nature,
Peered into the swift enfolding gloom.

Prognostic

There comes a moment late in Summer
When yellow pulses like a muffled bell,
A tremor foreboding the mortal stroke,
The first faltering of the chlorophyll.

This is not the yellow haunting the mind
In ghost of crocus, daffodil, lemon-bright
Forsythia, new butter of the daisy disk,
Yellow dissolving light, dissolved in light.

That airy yellow, cream yellow, flaxen yellow,
Spirit yellow washed pale gold by the Spring sun,
Together with flesh of primrose, jonquil, buttercup,
Has long since drowned in a heavy sea of green.

No, this yellow is waxen, tawny, buff,
Mottled gold of straw, wheat stalk, corn husk:
Darkness is a presence, fog an interfusion—
This is antique amber holding an inner dusk.

There comes a moment when thought reverberates
And yellow is a passing bell; indeed, tomorrow
Stains the world hectic, speckles it with red fever,
Then wastes and crumples it to dry brown sorrow.

As in a Watermark

As in a watermark, we read
Beneath the gloss of grass and weed
The obsolete foundation plan
And where the walls and plumbing ran.

Here the sunken stones secrete
The pathways of now vanished feet;
Each surviving trace contrives
To shroud the scars of former lives.

With ease we read the door was here,
But not the bygone shut-in fear;
We read the contours of this room,
But not its muffled private doom.

We read in this eclipsed debris
The leveling catastrophe;
Not Pompeii's crushing pantomime,
But the lava flow of time.

Pastoral

Beneath the hollow of the sky
The farmhouse stands secure,
With barn, shed, and pump nearby,
And great oak to shade the door.

By that wisp of smoke revealed,
The daily life proceeds,
Drawing from the circling field
All its daily needs.

But what is hidden is the web
Of finest filament,
Whose radiating finials stab
The farthest continent.

And though the spreading threads are frail
And unbelievably thin,
They can pull down this sheltering wall
To crush the life within.

Abstract Season

Stain and color, flush and fever
Bleach, blanch, drain away;
Fading leaf and grass uncover
Black, white, ash, and gray.

Blend and mingle, pied and dapple,
All that might equivocate,
Coiled and curved, soft and supple
Reduced to angled, stiff, and straight.

Full and rich, lush and ample
Wane and wither, strip the earth
Bare, hard, stark, simple:
Now comes the long-needed Birth.

East Wind

Which way the foul wind blows
Is from the east, from the east,
Chafing throat and pinching nose.

The east wind works in bleak grisaille;
Across gray skies, lead-gray tatters
Pelt down rain and iron hail.

Oh, let us have some other wind,
One that blows up no dirty papers
Along the gutters of the mind:

Not unbalance, not unmeasure,
But the west wind's balmy yellow,
Or the south wind's warming azure,

Even the north wind's white and clean
Single stroke of killing frost,
Sharp as the blade of the guillotine.

The Dream

Once again he found himself in that field
Whose four corners, lacking perspective, were square;
Bright flowers shone against its emerald
Like painted flowers glazed on earthenware.
Daisies, poppies, buttercups, marigolds, flags
(Some in that season should not have been blooming)
Threw their fresh colors on his bare arms and legs.

He rambled on toward hay stacked neat in cones,
While light untarnished tumbled in a torrent;
Within his flesh gleamed the lucid bones
(In that light all objects were transparent).
Stooping to study the death-cup of a toadstool,
He smiled to see his body cast no shadow
On his red heart beating gaily in its capsule.

A childish voice rang in the sparkling air:
"Red Rover, Red Rover, let Alice come over!"
As if waiting for some figure to appear,
A long moment he stood there in the clover,
Then turned and ran beyond the farthest stack.
My voice could not carry in that alien ether;
I knew, and yet I cried: "No! No! Come back! Come back!"

The field dissolved to alleys, twisted, narrow,
Where he trudged in soot damp and corrosive;
Across the cobbles limped a sickly sparrow,
The houses were familiarly oppressive.
Identity he had, could he but wash
From himself the strange ill-fitting body
Of brittle scaffold-bones and wilted flesh.

A swarthy radiance exuded from the sky.
Coming to a crossing, he stood there puzzled,
As if he knew not where he was, nor why.
He stared at his thin arms, the hair was grizzled;
All was murky, all things were now opaque.
He looked into his breast; the heart was hidden,
Its presence betrayed only by a deep ache.

He felt a wind come up, and he was driven
Like a hunted felon in some antique chromo.
Underneath the scene faint words were graven;
I put my glasses on, and read *Ecce homo!*
Just then a shrill falsetto screamed: "Run, sheep, run!"
Startled, the child-man recalled his mission,
Turned blindly down a lane, and stumbled on.

This August Sun

This August sun
Spreads its dye,
Burns beard of corn
Brown and dry,
Stains the apple,
Rounds the grape,
Presses the tomato
Into shape.

But tender sapling,
Blade of grass,
Beware this globe
Of molten brass;
Its scorching ray
Will drain each vein.
Pray for cloud
And balm of rain.

And squirrel, rabbit,
Panting fox,
Seek the shade
Of trees and rocks;
Hide behind,
Creep below,
Or be struck down
With one swift blow.

As I Was Walking Down Fifth Avenue

As I was walking down Fifth Avenue,
I came upon Summer trapped behind plate glass;
The roses were rose red, the sky was sky blue,
And the grass, the grass was green as grass.

And three enchanting women stood, immaculate,
On the green grass that would never need mowing,
Their dresses unruffled, the hem lines straight,
And not one slip was showing.

And two bronzed men sipped amber at a table,
A brand-new rake leaned against the nearby wall;
Off in the corner a child reached for a bauble,
And a little dog played with a colored ball.

And clean straw was there for hayride or barn dance,
All was ready, yes, eager, about to, on the verge;
Yet landscape and attitude were held in a trance—
And no mere window dresser the thaumaturge.

Frowning, I wondered why they had not the strength
To break so benign a spell; and as I paused there guessing,
The scene had depth and width and length,
I saw, but one dimension was missing.

For strangely there was no bark, no cry,
No pulsing at the throat or wrist,
No stir, no flicker on the sky-blue sky:
And Time must have sound and motion to exist.

And then it was, foreknowing Winter,
My heart ached to join that happy scene;
I knocked and called and tried to enter,
But more than plate glass stood between.

In a World of Giant Inches

Scurrying with private purpose,
Yet exercising proper caution,
This mite advances on my desk-top,
A grain of sand in locomotion.

Like the Lord's Prayer on a pinhead,
Crowded quarters; yet room quite ample
For legs and blood and nerves and stomach,
Apparatus far from simple.

A dot in a world of giant inches,
Yet room enough for vital magic,
Room for judgment and decision,
Even room for love and logic.

Indian Summer

Sit on this warm stone.
Now shut your eyes.
Let insect drone
Mesmerize
And heat of sun
Certify
The time is noon
Back in July.

Full of belief,
Open your eye
To harvest sheaf
And tarnished sky;
Enchanted sense
Cannot then blur
The evidence
Of the calendar.

Academic Tombstones

A Committee
They hem and haw in fields Elysian,
The buck is passed and then returned,
They cannot come to a decision—
They never died, they just adjourned.

A Stuffed Shirt
Once stripped of the distributions, curves, and trends,
The resounding voice, the mouth-filling terms,
The great names that were friends of friends of his friends,
Nothing was left for the worms.

A Monograph
Waiting to bring some bookish slave
A sleep as sound as the sleep of the just,
Duly clad in buckram grave,
It rests in peace and gathers dust.

A Cautious Professor
Trembling on the brink of dissolution,
This dust, marked by its old uncertainty,
Debates with feverish irresolution
To be or not to be.

The Critic's Lexicon

Hubris

See him put forth the peacock's plumage,
See the high arrogance in his stride,
As he proudly speaks the Greek word *Hubris*,
Which is the Greek word for *pride*.

Logos

Beats there a heart that has not stirred
To *Logos*, the Greek word for *word*!
It makes the critical circles buzz,
That's what the Greek word *Logos* does.

Reply to a Young Poet

You say you want the poem to be absolute You,
No crap (you say), no bilge, no flourishes.
You want to dig to the clear source that nourishes,
Every feeling honest, every image true.

You want the poem clean and hard as stone,
And yet to sing and soar like a bird;
To go back to what was in the beginning—the word,
And strip the word to the bone.

Then will the word speak with its elemental force,
No echo from the Past, no tampering by Art.
I understand: Everything straight, straight from the heart!
Of course! Of course! Of course, of course, of course!

Well, suppose you cut the poem down to a single word—let's
    say Rain:
No two rains are alike, falling out of no two skies,
No two moments observed by no two eyes,
Aside from all the hanky-panky in the brain.

Or say you get the poem down to the number 1:
Even that simple 1, stared at long enough,
Puts forth a foliage of outlandish stuff
And dances off into the blinding sun.

So babble or grunt, hack away with a knife,
Turn all your working hours into Judgment Days:
You can write a poem in as many ways
As you can live a life.

Discourse on the Real

The shades are half-drawn on classroom and hall
Now deserted but for the ghostly babel
Left by the celebrants in the perennial miracle
Of Alphabet and Multiplication Table.
On a back door, to *épater le bourgeois*,
One Summer infidel has fixed the taunting scribble:
School is over school is over ha ha ha!

Not long since the schoolyard cradled a little nation,
The sole material residue of former act and cry
Being the crumpled dusty wrappers in gentle gyration
Of Baby Ruth, Wild Cherry Gum, and Eskimo Pie.
But off there, sunlight and air currents beget swarms
Of leaping shapes and phantoms to trick the eye,
A whirling dance of Platonic Forms.

And now I make out Coquetry in a dress's flutter,
And Love strolls hand-in-hand along the walks;
There Indecision goes up and down on the teeter-totter,
And Master Builder raises castles in the sandbox.
Exhibition throws himself from ring to ring,
While False Modesty stands aside and mutely mocks,
And Dreamer rides to Graustark on her private swing.

The sun strikes untold colors from the playground pebbles.
I shake the fictive from my head: the schoolhouse brick
Is plain and real and solid, fact not fable—
No need for Dr. Johnson's confirming kick.
And yet, I think, the filling matter is the fiction,
The leaping shapes and phantoms not a trick;
Perhaps we find the real in the abstraction.

Always there will be the new First Grader,
Although the singular flesh that took the mold
Has gone down the years wiser and sadder:
The forms are always with us waiting to be filled.
And always the bushes screening the steps conceal
The ever-present Platonist sitting there, beguiled
By which of this is fiction, which is real.

In the House and Out

The wind is rising this troubled night,
Plucking at the timbers of the house,
Trying each chink, each fault
For a place to take hold with tearing hand.
But the house will stand.
It was firmly built.
Custom gave it a strong and supple structure,
All the concealed cunning of stress and strain;
And discretion taught it not to fracture,
But sway to the thrust and twist of the storming air.
The timbers groan, they will not be shaken loose.
Now comes the searching rain.
Yet I have no fear.
The house is tight,
The house will stand.

Out in the woods behind the house,
Where the trees cavort and turn and bend
To the urgency of rain and wind,
Can be heard the crash
Of some living thing beating through the underbrush;
A thing perhaps with hoof or snout,
Perhaps clawed and tailed,
Caught in a maze where it can find no path, no sky,
Only confusion, tumult, falling branch, tangling vine,
Lost, lost, lost, and seeking a way out;
Made cruel and wild
By wind, rain, and solid night.
I hear it whimper and cry.
(Why is there something familiar about the voice?)

Perhaps a lightning flash or St. Elmo's light
Will pierce the thickset black,
And the pale mushrooms and things not green
Will even by the most frantic be seen
Glowing in the sunless corner of the oak.
Perhaps the quivering nose or groping fingertip
Will feel the velvet of the moss—
Not true north, but a useful approximation—and thus find
A way through lash and whip
Into the clear and open field.

The Wood of the Self-Destroyers

—DANTE, *Hell*, Canto 13

We enter the dismal wood where boughs black,
Gnarled, and thorny cradle the fouled nests
From which the harpies swoop to crunch and crack
Those wretches who jump to streets, slash their wrists,
Inhale exhaust fumes, gulp the sleeping pills,
Drink the lysol and tear their burning breasts.
Our eyes grow used: the gloom but half conceals
Those who welcome sickness, cut off an ear,
And to ease the inward sore gorge and swill;
Who waste in apathy or cynic sneer,
Always deny and in denial smart,
Subvert the self by coward lie or fear,
And solitary, crouching each apart,
Snuffle *No! No!* to proffered hand and heart.

For Ground-Hog Day

Let there be light
Of such candor
That no shadow blight
Behind and under.

Or let the soul
Be so pervasive
That no substance unroll
The dark missive.

Let both be one,
Or either be widow:
But we are undone
By substance *and* shadow.

Narcissus

The bulb here planted
Winter deep
Will sleep an enchanted
Hedgehog sleep.
While ice and snow
Stab and maim,
The bulb below
Will forge a dream.

A rare transaction
Will be done:
The calefaction
Of the sun
Unfold a petal
Paper-white,
Frail and subtle,
To rival light.

Spring Thaw

Stoop to the ground and look close.
This miniature dam lies shattered;
Crumbs of earth and shreds of grass,
An hour ago cemented with ice,
Now all scattered.

See in this water particle,
Creeping along its capillary,
Brook and stream and river swell,
And curdled torrent sweeping all
To the estuary.

Hear in this hidden muted trickle
The flooded rapids boom and thunder,
Trees and dikes and houses crackle,
The hiss and roar as steep banks buckle,
Cut from under.

Autumn Equinox

Now neither night
Nor day prevails,
And one hair might
Turn the scales.
In this thin
Moment's trance,
Earth cannot spin,
Nor Time advance.

Poised to fall
Are pear and apple,
The green hedge-wall
About to topple.
The leaf is now
On the verge,
And naked bough
Must soon emerge.

Locust hum
Gives way to hush:
But Ruin will come
With a rush,
The wild bird shriek
Upset the balance.
Oh, cruel beak
And iron talons!

Old Spanish Song

Estos mis cabellicos, madre;
Dos á dos me los lleva el aire.

Leaf and old paper race by together,
The edge of the year is beginning to fray,
And these fair hairs on my head, mother,
Two by two the wind blows them away.

Promise and dream whirl off in tatters,
The fading sun slants to the gust,
The shutter bangs, the weatherboard clatters,
The gourd on its vine scrapes in the dust.

This is it, there will be no other:
The tempest tears at the ends of the day,
And these fair hairs on my head, mother,
Two by two the wind blows them away.

Exercise in Pessimism

What rhymes with hope?
Not dawn, not dream,
Not star, nor gleam,
But grope and dope,
And mope and rope:
That rhymes with hope.

What rhymes with wish?
Not love, not health,
Not fame, nor wealth,
But squish and swish,
Poor fish and pish:
That rhymes with wish.

What rhymes with life?
Not joy, not long,
Not wine, nor song,
But fife and knife,
And strife with wife:
That rhymes with life.

And so for truth,
The rhyme is tooth;
And for tomorrow,
The rhyme is sorrow.
Then lose not your season
Seeking reason,
Nor waste your time
To find a rhyme.

To the First Robin

Remember, fair-weather friend,
You fled across the border
And left us to contend
With cold-blooded murder.

When the low sky like a stone
Lay heavy on our heart,
When trees stripped to the bone,
You chose then to desert.

But now that the calendar
Brings a breathing space,
You pipe a note of cheer
And show your shameless face.

Yet happy to be alive,
And full of bonhomie,
We foolishly forgive
Your canting perfidy.

Do Not in This House Mock

Do not in this house mock
Each makeshift compromise;
Think what may provoke
The need to improvise.

See the perfect plan
Warp, skew, and twist,
Making Visionary Man
Man the Empiricist.

Sit before the grate,
Gaze into the flames,
And there contemplate
The shape of former dreams.

The measure of my joy
Take by sun, snow, and rain
In ever-changing play
Across the windowpane.

And tread light upon the floor:
By that cracked board's groan,
Know Grief the rude visitor
Cut me to the bone.

Journal Entry

Set down wind direction, velocity;
Note if sky was overcast, sunlight slack.
Eschewing fable and hyperbole,
Write the strict data of the almanac.
Record what came to bloom, what went to seed,
Where you journeyed, whom you met, what you did;
Inscribe the positive for all to read—
Memento clear-cut as a pyramid.

But how find the symbol, sign, number, word
To name the panic in the thickened air,
The ambuscade behind the naked face,
The warning indistinctly overheard?
How solve the lost riddle revealing where
Forgotten shaft meets secret burial place?

These Are the Hands

These are the hands that will fail me,
And these are the eyes;
These are the feet that will falter,
And this the heart;
These lungs will not hold enough breath
To stain a glass;
Each tube, each valve, each hinge
Will come apart.

This jelly of starch and albumen
Will shrink and collapse;
Where now this order prevails,
There then will be
No balance of fuel against ash,
No growth, no repair,
But another, a different kind
Of chemistry.

Circe

The poison lay not in her but them.
What form their appetite would take
She never knew: she dreamed of flame,
Or waterfall, or mountain peak.

Or if a beast, then unicorn,
Stag, and stallion came to mind.
Thus dreaming, yet fearing what she'd learn,
She sighed and touched them with her wand.

And once again, all, all was lost
As snout and bristles began to bud:
She flung them acorns, berries, mast;
They shed tears and rooted in the mud.

They Say the *Last Supper* Is Badly Damaged

(1945)

They say the Last Supper is badly damaged—
Leonardo's, and valued at one asterisk.
They say the Renaissance sprawls on the Arno in ruins,
And St. Stephen's stands a charred and roofless husk.

Each antique name descends in a shower of souvenirs.
There are questions to ask. One asks, recalls, and ponders.
Will the rubble core of the city mock the map etched in the brain?
The feet by some habit of the bone find their way among the cinders?

And do you remember on the far side of the Isar a phantom village in
the mist?
How in Coblenz we ate on a terrace overhanging the Rhine, with the
bees at the honey?
What we sought was always in the next street just around the corner.
Do you remember? Let us take a guided tour with our hearts as
cicerone.

There were people too, were there not? And where are they?
Rafael? Anna? Denise? (Last seen going east, destination a
crematorium.)
Micki and Blanca? Think. Yes, think. Each, each, each was a person.
Jacques? Margit? Hans? Erna? And who was left to sing the requiem?

They say once upon a time shepherdesses made love at Versailles,
In Florence Dante dreamed his medieval dream,
And the Lorelei haunted a rock beneath the painted castles.
Once upon a time. Say it again. *Once upon a time.*

That siren strain lured us like Odysseus.
And though Time had got there first, we could not rest.
Somewhere were the magic words—perhaps hidden in the fine print
of Baedeker;
Not yet had we been forced to conclude that this Europe did not exist.

Thus we wandered through a mansion of many and elegant chambers.
There must have been a price, but we never asked who paid.
Behind the wainscoting we never discovered the bones
Thrown there by arrogance, privilege, and time-honored greed.

Now the enchantment has rubbed away, we stumble in a gutted cellar
Where lurks the feudal horror with its pimps and its obscenities.
Through the gloom we see the immemorial masonry of broken bodies,
And in the binding mortar the eyes, the hopeless eyes, the terror-
    stricken eyes.

Summer Interlude

This hushed glade hidden in the city park
Gathers the morning sunlight in a pocket.
Across the rows of chairs bent to an arc
The empty band shell, like an eyeless socket,
Holds all the local spirits in a trance,
The silence broken only by a cricket
And the cicada's undulating sibilance.

The grass has sprung back; I see no trace
Of last night's footsteps. One butterfly hovers,
A white petal accenting the emptiness.
And now a slender passing cloud covers
The glade with a film through which the sun bleeds.
A moment since, it seems, parents, lovers,
Children stole off into the nearby woods.

Two observers are here: I shut *my* eye
(Let the band shell reflect the vacant spaces).
On my inner lid grows a star-flecked sky,
And floodlights catch the attentive faces.
My head begins to nod and sway; a waltz
Swings in my ear, and high above the brasses
The lyric clarinet descants and lilts.

I see. I hear. And then I smell the sweat,
The rank perfume, the sickly sweet aroma
Of crackerjack, the acrid cigarette.
My eyes open once more to the old dilemma:
What part of this will stay? What part will change?
Which is waking? Which, universal coma?
Which is the familiar? And which the strange?

Band shell, chairs, and one white butterfly
Poise before me as if captivated,
When all at once from the nearby woods a cry
Betrays some grief or passion consummated.
Tonight, one will slip in with transfixed stare
To join his fellow men here congregated,
And silent lovers will steal back pair by pair.

Today's Horoscope

Indications are for a day of conflict and indecision,
With the emotions held in check by a rather sluggish state of mind.
Watch your step. Travel at your own risk.
Be on your guard against agreements or promises of any kind.

All documents should be sound and clear to the understanding.
Make certain of the details. Take heed of all particulars.
Direct the mentality always into safe channels.
There are prognostications of disaster in the stars.

Safeguard the possessions against unforeseen loss;
Stocks and bonds and other securities may fall.
Protect the reputation and domestic well-being from treachery.
Beware of whatever is out there in the hall.

Those whose birthday it is may encounter a year
Of contradictory situations. Take no unwarranted chances.
Keep to your side of the street. Look both ways before crossing.
Preserve your balance. Refrain from all extravagances.

A child born on this day may have generous impulses,
With hopes and ambitions beyond his talents or means.
Part of him will never laugh. There is cause for alarm.
Let him look under beds, and behind doors and screens.

Be apprehensive of all relations with man, woman, or child.
Let not the smile spread to the eyes. Surrender that dream.
When you wake the world will be changed.
The conjunction of the planets is inauspicious in the extreme.

Tomorrow's Horoscope

Indications are for a day of promise and fulfillment,
With the cosmic shadows held in check by friendly vibrations.
Events will be exciting. Keep your head in the clouds.
Your achievements will exceed your fondest hopes and expectations.

All matters of business and romance are aspected favorably.
Energize your ambitions. Be aggressive. Be of good cheer.
Propitious influences are at work. Ride the crest of the wave.
There can be no reason to regret. Break the shackles of fear.

Consider that this day begins your cycle of happiness.
Open your mail. Clean out your bureau drawer.
People of affluence and means will be well disposed toward you.
Go bargain hunting. You will find just what you are looking for.

Those whose birthday it is will encounter a year
Of dynamic opportunities. Be on the alert for good news.
The ground will not crumble beneath your feet.
Let down your guard. You can't possibly lose.

A child born on this day will win his heart's desire.
His personality will skyrocket him to fortune and fame.
People will envy him. He will be the life of the party.
For him there can be no hardship, no disappointment, no shame.

You will wake in the morning and remember nothing of the night.
The occult is your ally. Put aside your anxiety.
Ask and it will be yours, whatever you say.
Oh, what will it be? Oh, what will it be, what will it be?

Lullaby

Proverbs 24:33

All day you have been a fierce stranger,
Alarming the enemy near and far.
Leave now that land of strife and danger,
Come back where things seem what they are.
The last glow flickers in the ember;
Return from field and dungeon-keep.
The time has come for a little slumber,
A little folding of the hands to sleep.

You have been gone in some rare city
Playing hero, monster, prince, buffoon;
Discarding guises without pity
And leaving masks in the alleys strewn.
Dusk turns night, and thoughts grow somber;
Pile toys and costumes in a heap.
The time has come for a little slumber,
A little folding of the hands to sleep.

Palette for April

Yellow for bright,
For sun-burst, sun-spill,
For signal light
Of crocus and daffodil.

Violet for shy,
For demure, for startle,
For timorous eye
Of hyacinth and myrtle.

Green for hope,
For slender, for brief,
For tentative shape
Of bud and leaf.

Pink and white for flesh
To cover, to blur,
For cherry blush
And flowering pear.

Gray and black for bone,
For brittle, for crunch,
For skeleton stone,
Trunk, and branch.

To Make a Crèche

This is a time for naïveté,
For innocence, for gay unreason;
And some things on this holiday
Should be out of place and out of season.

Plant olive or holly or mistletoe,
Indeed, whatever you are able.
Use tinsel for ice, cotton for snow,
And then set down the open stable.

And carve the figures plain and crude:
Shepherds, Magi, oxen, sheep.
Determine each artless attitude;
Let some be awake and some be asleep.

And at the center of all, compose
Joseph and Mary, and the little stranger
Wrapped there in his swaddling clothes,
Lying there in his manger.

And hang a star high above
To serve the coming year as trope
For the imperative of love,
The necessity of hope.

Heirloom

The heirloom (you tell me) has come down to us
From your Old Country grandmother on your father's side.
Or was it great-grandmother? Well, no need to fuss.
About its provenance (to use the scholar's term)
The scholar will have to remain unsatisfied.

But what exactly *is* it? It does not defy
Description, and yet it is a hybrid artifact.
No doubt, *somewhere* there must be a name to call it by:
A small three-legged pan-handled shallow iron pot;
The iron thickly rusted, the enamel lining badly cracked.

And what was it used for? About that we can only guess.
It must have stood three-legged on hot coals or an open fire.
After all, the possibilities are not limitless.
It is much too small for meat or vegetables, even soup;
Perhaps porridge to pacify some infant crier.

Of course, you can conjure up almost any kind of scene,
Fancies throng to the mind without end:
Humble hut, glittering palace, anything between.
As for characters and plot, it is all a matter
Of how much disbelief you are willing to suspend.

Sentimental value, yes. But no museum piece,
Nothing fashioned of precious stones and gold
By some pandering artist pampering some pampered caprice.
Nor is it an antique; even family legend
Hazards no more than a hundred years old.

But it has the beauty which human use gives a thing.
Whoever made it did no more than was needed:
Simple maker, crude object, homely virtues, chastening
That vain Egyptian—what *was* his name?—
And the monstrous vanity of his pyramid.

Ancestral Portraits

I see no bearded Hebrew patriarch
In some illuminated manuscript,
Clad in gold breastplate, ephod, mitre—mark
Of Aaron's sons—with somber face tight-lipped,
Aglow with sacred destiny; whose dim
Forefather spoke with the Lord of Creation
On Sinai's hill, and was ordained by Him
A kingdom of priests and a holy nation.
I see no broidered robe, no precious stones,
But this spat-upon Jewish gabardine
Cloaking a frail cowering skin-and-bones
In a Polish ghetto, dark and unclean.
I read in this sick countenance's gray
The harsh dichotomy of We and They.

Denied both pride of place and pride of name,
He wears for treasured heirloom, boast of birth,
A malignant gem, an old badge of shame.
Thy seed shall be as the dust of the earth,
Promised the Lord.—Yes, as dust blindly tossed
Into the whirlwind. This grim irony
Could best be savored by one who had lost
In the Diaspora his ancestry.
Fury-driven, scattered through evil-eyed
Proud alien peoples, everywhere he knew
A hate more ancient than their foolish pride.
Thus was he chosen and thus made a Jew,
Not by crazed myths of race or blood or creed,
But bitter suffering and dire need.

To this cold Northland, far from fig and palm,
His fleeing forebears came. I hear them weep,
Each night crying the cry of David's psalm:

I will both lay me down in peace, and sleep.
Around the edges of the Euxine Sea,
From Morocco into the Spanish trap,
Through the crooked alleys of Germany,
I trace their wanderings on this mute map.
Had this map but a tongue, what might it tell
Of hopeless staggering from place to place,
Of desperate means and aching farewell,
Of all the tortured seepage of a race?
Who said "a rootless people" said in vain;
They sank their roots deep in the soil of pain.

Thou preparedst a table before him,
Oh Lord, in the presence of his enemies,
Heaped with dust and sour ashes to the rim.
His heart, cramped by ceaseless anxieties,
Quivers to the oblique glance, the slight,
The sneer—dread portents of shattered quiet,
Savage curse, bestial howl in the tiger night
Aflame with the pogrom's frenzied riot.
How the mere word can hatch maggots that teem
Within the guilty lesion of the soul,
Veiled fears bodied as in the purging dream,
Foul creatures creeping from the mind's bunghole!—
Phantoms? Vain conjurings?—Once you have heard
"Jew!" hissed, then doubt the power of the word!

Perhaps you find this portrait incomplete.
Where are the hands? you ask. The mouth and hair?—
Obliterated by time's winding-sheet
Long since.—Is he tall or short? Dark or fair?
Does he have this one's forehead? That one's nose?—
Dead silence.—This much can be said: the print
Of grief, the morbid uncertainty shows

In the fringes of the eye.—One more hint:
This portrait should be done in Rembrandt's style—
Faint lights, swart shadows, sober coloring;
The skull's flesh-and-blood, lightened by no smile,
Like an apparition; while menacing
In the background, fitful brute figures lurk,
Half-extinguished by the glimmering murk.

II

Even as a child, her dark and grave eyes—
Not the child's mirrors easy to divert—
Wear the light of sunset, not of sunrise,
The long anxious brooding on some deep hurt.
The careless laughter of a tender age
In her is underscored by something sad;
In all her girlish play lurks something sage,
She has a heart not readily made glad.
Through the cloud of years I see this ghetto maid
Tread the twisted lane of a medieval hive.
Her skin is fresh, her hair coiled in a braid;
Northern girls ripen late, but she soon grows,
Biding the single duty of her life,
From folded bud to Sharon's full-blown rose.

One day she wed.—Here, in an alien tongue,
I tell once more the tale of Rachel, told
Long ago; once more sing Solomon's song.
For this, I plunder that treasure of gold
Minted by crabbed scholars in King James's day:
Oh, like jewels are the joints of her thighs!
Rise up, oh love, oh fair one, and come away!
Yes, a garden enclosed is she!—He lies
All night betwixt her breasts, and his left hand
Under her head, his right embracing her.

He kisses her with the kisses of his mouth.
He is come into his garden. The drouth
Is ended. Her hands drop with sweet-smelling myrrh,
And the voice of the turtle is heard in the land.

Behold then her fierce resolve to annul
Her proud maiden beauty! She shaves the bright
Prized tresses from her head and bares the skull,
As the humbling wont of the Israelite
Prescribes. Thus self-abased, she meekly wears
The ordained coif to hide the naked bone.
Can we now grasp what this cruel act declares?—
She cleaves to one man, and one man alone.
Not like the tight-choking vine does she cleave,
But leans on him and lets him lean on her,
His comforter and sweet idolater.
His love is breath itself: her sole desire,
That all their living moments interweave,
And then their dust fuse in the grave's slow fire.

Were this a novel, each particular
Might be recorded in fine rhetoric—
The wretched progress of her calendar,
The births, the deaths, the nursing of the sick;
The close-knit web of smell and sight and sound,
The day-to-day events, the cares, the brief
Fading interludes of joy quickly drowned
In the consuming gloom of man's common grief.
Man's common grief, and more! She dwells apart
On an island hard beset by danger,
And living as the Jew must live, withdrawn,
Always the pariah, the loathed stranger.
Her hours are measured by her troubled heart —
And soon the days, the weeks, the years are gone.

Unheralded, a widowed crone in black
Appears one day where once a shy girl stood,
With a thick host of phantoms at her back.
But yesterday she shed her maidenhood;
But yesterday that joyous sacrifice
Of her first-born son at the circumcision.
She now knows the extorted bleeding price
Paid for time's smallest fugitive division.—
What perverse spell brought this transformation?
From what tissue did these gnarled hands emerge?
Whence came this wrinkled skin and infirm flesh?—
Her children scattered in humiliation,
Her ear echoing with her husband's dirge,
She awaits the hound straining at the leash.

Flower Arrangement

These flowers in their symmetry
Beat back the cosmic anarchy.
No commotion do they feel
From drift of sun or earth's wild reel.

Balanced here are hue and stain,
Light and shadow, curve and plane:
Nothing here is left to chance,
And change is here held in a trance.

But look! Come close! All is not tight.
Marauder ant and petal blight
Drop speckles of betraying dust.
See on this leaf the touch of rust!

In Time of War

Here in this garden,
With no forewarning,
Summer lays down its delicate barrage
From earliest morning,
With bird notes for fusillade,
And crackling twig for artillery,
Machine-gun rattle of the woodpecker,
Zooming of the bee,
Flare of the corolla,
The dragonfly's menacing drone,
Distant drumfire of the rain,
Clatter of the thunderstone.
The lethal fragrance of the lily
Holds the senses in its power
Here in this garden;
Yet here, here Man need not cower,
Neither need he brave death
With his last poor breath.

The Offering

My brother came to me,
Holding his heart in his hand.
I looked at it ruthlessly,
I observed it contract and expand.

I examined the cunning construction
Of the delicate doors and the walls.
I studied the singular action,
Each flutter, twitch, and pulse.

The heart, as I watched it, halted:
Its manner grew furtive and shy.
It sought to hide (I exulted),
It shivered under my eye.

But why was my own heart raw?
Why did it tremble and whine?
In my brother's hand, I then saw,
The heart which he held was mine.

The Vine

You cover me with fragrant bloom—
Sprigs of honeyed word,
Leaves of scented courtesy.
Bedecked am I from head to toe.
Thus brilliantly arrayed, bestrewn
With blossom, tendril, and festoon,
I think to stalk in majesty
Like some gorgeous jungle bird.

But what is this that will not let me go?
What wire, creeping, serpentine,
Cuts my flesh, binds my bone?
Whence came this strangling vine?

Dr. Eliot's New Five-Foot Shelf

"What you think about depends on what you eat and not on the books you read," declared Dr. T. C. Barnes of the Hahnemann Medical College, Philadelphia, in the course of a paper on the physiological basis for the electrical activity of the brain.

—*News item*

Our thought comes not from Aristotle,
But from traffic epiglottal;
Seek not ideas in Machiavelli,
Just put something in your belly.
That pensiveness is not Racine,
But a Portuguese sardine;
And that scorn is not Voltaire,
But a piece of sharp Gruyère.
That platitude from Dr. Johnson?
Just a headcheese from Wisconsin.
That wit from Sir John Suckling?
Merely roast Long Island duckling.
That morbidness is not John Donne,
But a hamburger on bun;
Nor is that allegory Bunyan,
Rather the added slice of onion.
That criticism Shaw?
No, just a carrot eaten raw.
And that mysticism Blake?
Simply a rare sirloin steak.
At least we cannot be mistaken
That our logic comes from Bacon;
And that brilliant epigram,
We can be sure it comes from Lamb.

Early Morning Moon

Pallid timepiece out of time,
Victim of an ill-matched race
Caught in an unavailing climb,
We read your future in your face.

With finer thread than spiders spin,
Drag the ocean in a fold;
Soon the hunter closing in
Drowns your silver in his gold.

Sing a plaintive minor strain;
While you may, be faintly heard,
Before the lion shakes his mane
And roars the fatal word.

Lift White Petal

Lift white petal and behold
The wilderness on this plant:
See aphid ravage leaf,
And small ant murder ant.

Stare into rat's bead-eye
Behind that hollyhock.
Touch iron in the rose,
Velvet on the rock.

For Christmas *1963*

These white faces North and South,
With glare for eye, gape for mouth,
Contorted not by the TV screen,
But by the mind's lesion, the heart's gangrene!

How can Justice, Good, even Shame dispel
The snarl, the jeer, the screech, the yell?
How plead with those who ululate?
How reason with this unreasoned hate?

Our need, our need is for everything mild,
For mercy, love, Mother and Child.
That heavenly host, where is it then,
Saying: *On earth peace, good will toward men?*

The Middle Distance

You sit up high in jet comfort, six miles high,
Cruising (the captain announces) point-eight-five the speed of sound:
Fantastic! Though not exactly a tea tray in the sky!
For sound if it wishes can still catch up,
And you can still make it (you hope) back to the ground.

Far far below you a relief map unrolls, precise, to scale:
The patchwork quilt of fields not quite square,
Rivers, lakes, valleys, hills, the colors pale;
And across the plains, even through the wildest Rockies,
The highways in straight lines going Lord-knows-where.

You cannot, of course, see men. But you can see Man:
His mark is there despite mountain, desert, swamp, cataract;
His farm to live on, his town to dwell in, his road to go by, his bridge
    to span.
And on that grandiose stage, as in a morality play,
His virtues grandly strut and declaim in the abstract.

You need to be close to see the blood and sweat,
The tears, the payment paid, the *quid pro quo;*
All there to be read, if you have learned the alphabet,
Written on the faces in the lines that line them,
The look between husband and wife, friend and friend, foe and foe.

Yes, you need to be very far or very near:
It is the middle distance which is blind,
It is the middle distance which cannot hear,
The middle distance knows neither men nor Man,
The middle distance has neither heart nor mind.

Those with the Bright Hard Faces

Jeremiah 36:18

As they came out from their secret places
I met those with the bright hard faces,
But under the garments they wore
I put my hand on the sore.

I read each frantic appeal
On the scribbled tablets that fell
From the anguished hands as they shook,
And I wrote them with ink in the book.

I heard the beat of the blood
Thundering its inquietude,
I took note of the habit of eye,
The cheekbones were hectic and dry.

I read and unraveled each spell
In the veins of the leaves that fell
From the tree of wrath as it shook,
And I wrote them with ink in the book.

Winter Landscape

Here is no vast fantastic glacier
Flowing and yet iron-hard,
Condensing plural forms by pressure
To single vacancy unmarred.

Here lies a small heart in whose brittle
Chambers red converts to blue:
Not weight of snow, but a subtle
Hammer stamps out blocks of dew.

And now behold within the shrinking
Arteries the ice, how bright!
And hear the sharp crystals clanking
As they cataract into night.

These Clay Tablets

These clay tablets betray what man once willed—
Brittle tokens of long-departed sounds
That slipped from trembling blood-lined throats and filled
Towns now sleeping under the silent mounds.
These wedge-shaped scratches expose the dead past,
Or so we say. In them we read men's acts:
Goods bought and sold, gain and loss, wealth amassed,
Taxes, titles, deeds, nothing but the facts.

The facts! The facts! Is there the life revealed?
Some hand recorded these shipments of grain.
It shook with what fury? Clenched with what pain?
And the man chose which dim passage since sealed
By time? Did he meet with the phantom he sought?
Was he nearer journey's end than he thought?

Read This Face

Be forewarned:
Seek not to spy
Through aperture
Of mouth or eye,
Nor be misled
By this benign
Calligraphy
Of crease and line.

The integument
Is thin but tough,
Each smallest muscle
Puncture-proof.
And inner craft
Knows what it reveals;
Read this face
By what it conceals.

To Make a Sunset

Scatter a handful of dust
With no premeditated scheme;
Rely on thrust and counter-thrust
Of vapor, speck, refracted beam.

Let the check of mist and cloud
Be your bold apocalypt;
Above the earth unroll the proud
Illuminated manuscript.

And there it is at close of day,
A mute chromatic testament,
The sun's diffused enchanted ray
Splashed across the firmament.

Tree of Knowledge

To these boughs the petals cling,
Jewels secreting perfume,
Charming the senses, promising
More days than time can consume.

The pink and sparkling white soon fade,
The bloom gives place to leaf,
Green contentment, quiet shade;
The sweet-scented days grow brief.

In stealth the harvest we awaited
Was nourished at the root;
The tree at last has borne the fated
Strange and bitter fruit.

And knowledge thriftily was stored
Against a certain day;
The tree is now a flaming sword
Turning every way.

Agenbite of Inwit

The behavior of *Ameba* in the
absence of external stimuli, for
example when it is suspended
freely in the water, shows that
some of its activities are initiated
by internal causes. Whether or
not the animal is in any degree
conscious is a question still un-
answered.

—R. W. HEGNER,
An Introduction to Zoology

Perhaps within this outer
Broods the conscious inner,
Lost in thought, tormented,
A microscopic sinner.

Crying *mea culpa*,
And wearing a horsehair shirt
Next to its protoplasm,
Kneels the introvert.

The Sad Lot of Henry Fielding

Henry Fielding. Praised by Boswell, Gibbon, Coleridge, Hazlitt, Lamb, and Byron; disparaged by Johnson, Smollett, De Quincey, Carlyle, and Browning.

—M. N. NEEDLEMAN AND W. B. OTIS,
An Outline-History of English Literature since Milton

The praises of Boswell, Coleridge, Lamb,
Byron, Hazlitt, and Gibbon
Would make life a basket of comfits and jam
Done up in satin and ribbon,
Were it not for the presence of Johnson, Carlyle,
De Quincey, Smollett, and Browning,
Full of disparagement, malice, and bile,
Off in the corner and frowning.

Today Each Sign

Today each sign is on its guard,
No cloudy emblem to be read:
Surfaces are clear and hard,
Blue enamel overhead.

I find myself in a tidy street,
All simple as a monorail;
Nothing to deflect my feet,
No significant detail.

Those I meet are sheathed in tile,
The teeth between their lips bright
In the cultivated smile
Tempest-proof and watertight.

Surfaces are hard and clear,
No hint of film, crack, or bruise.
How catch a glimpse? How overhear?
How find the clues? How find the clues?

Second-Act Intermission

Not beside us here in the haze of cigarette smoke,
Nor lurking in the splinters of brittle talk,
But back there, behind the curtain, standing in the wing,
The enigma awaits its nightly unraveling.

The silver cord cut when the curtain descended,
We are shapes flickering in a fog, suspended
Between two compelling worlds as in a transparent sheath;
Beyond those open doors people draw a different breath.

Those passing by in the street, adrift just outside the doors,
They are not of us. They have not shed our equivocal tears.
They do not know what we know. They have not eyes to read
With our sagacity the predicament that lies ahead.

For them there will be no adroit all-resolving third act,
Only the clutter of the infrangible iron fact;
No dramatic need will contain the catastrophe
Spilling over into the dim reaches of anxiety.

Not the neat situation of the calculated plot,
But the tangled strands of the knot
Whose trailing ends are lost, lost, irretrievably lost
In the riddle of the womb and the durance of the past.

From the suffocating hug of frustration, no release;
No shrinking from the slow abrasion of hopelessness;
No *deus ex machina* in time to put things right;
No ennobling death to bring relief each troubled night.

Those passing by in that street, in that outer gloom,
Will yearn for the right word in vain; it will not will not come.
Their movements will be clumsy, their gestures inept;
In vain they will look for the cue in the prepared script.

Off to the right Broadway can be sensed; its neon glare
Throws spectral red and blue and green across the outer air;
The rattle of a bus is pierced by the warning bell, whereupon
We return to meet the inevitable paid-for denouement.

March

The battle rages,
The heaven guns slam,
The lion rampages
Against the lamb.

The elements contend,
The clouds ricochet;
Sun wars on wind,
Blue wars on gray.

Water, long held under
In the clutch of a vise,
With savage thunder
Now shatters the ice.

And who puts ear
To earth's frozen peel
Can there plainly hear
Root ring on steel.

Autumn Forecast

Each tree is now a poppyhead,
Painted bronze and gold and red
As in some antique Book of Hours;
Leaves fall not leaves, but gaudy flowers.

One day a ragged sky will stare
Through twigs and branches plundered bare,
And only pine, spruce, and fir be seen
As tufts and plumes of blackened green.

Then the naked woods will grow
A thick and shaggy fleece of snow,
Into which trunk and branch will shrink,
And twigs will waste to lines of ink.

But trunk and branch and twig will stay
Against another day,
When Spring will kindle greenish glints
And sing a song of starts and hints.

Archaeological Footnote

From the crumbling crater edge, you and I survey pots, pans,
And such indices of progress as broken shoes and tires
Embedded in a matrix of clinkers and battered tin cans,
All burning to rust in time's deliberate fires.

Was that the wind or a rat? Trickles of sand cataract,
And another segment of a great civilization is hidden:
This is the magic transforming rubbish to artifact,
And city dump to treasure-yielding midden.

Some numbered sunsets gone by, and behold the centipedes
And the petrified tree stump where sits a raw-necked vulture,
Sole monarch of the flat waste and the prickly weeds
Flourishing grotesquely on our buried culture.

Then creeping over the horizon across the sifting sand
Come men with pick and shovel, a learned crew
Dispatched, no doubt, by the University of Tongaland
Or the Occidental Institute of Timbuktu.

And as they industriously dig and scrabble,
What frauds they reconstruct out of this debris—
Not *our* talk, but some irrelevant gabble,
Not *our* love, but some triumph of pedantry.

Gnarled Oak

Recorded here
In knob and ball,
The chronicle
Of bug and gall;

The sharp protest
Of scar and stain,
Against the stress
Of wind and rain;

In branch and twist,
The antiphon
To the strong tug
Of the sun;

Spasmodic spurt
And sudden halt,
In response
To soil and salt;

Outer pressure,
Inner need,
Recorded here
For us to read.

War Bride

Reluctantly her English feet forswear
The twisting lane, the up-and-down;
And are prevailed on by straight line and square
In this flat Midwestern town.

Upon her ear the words fall harsh and plain,
The syllables reveal each joint;
Remembered lilt, familiar pitch and strain
Echoing as counterpoint.

Her heart, its rhythm fixed in other places
Where it might beat without alarm,
Must learn these strange, stiff, angular faces,
These alien gestures mean no harm.

Her eyes shrink from this hard untempered light,
They seek the misted scenes of youth—
Until tears well up and blur their sight.
So tears once stood in the eyes of Ruth.

Actaeon

Naked Diana rises into sight.
In vain his troubled eye turns modestly:
Look where he will, the sleek flesh glistens white.
He sees what mortal man is not to see.

Oh, instant change! Manhood is forfeited.
Against the thin rib-wall the wild heart pounds;
It knows the furry horns sprung from his head,
And at his back the snuffling of the hounds.

Who are these hounds? Why does each put on the face
Of nameless dread? And was the name once known?
Was his own sore-pinched breast their secret lair?

Hot breath is on his flanks. The pack gives chase.
One hound he never sees, but senses there,
Is first to sink its fangs in his neck bone.

Winter's Tale

Silent snow has fallen all the night.
At last, at last the tardy dawn
Drags iron-gray over the field
And uncovers the white page
Waiting expectant for the day's signature.

Yet even at dawn the page is not blank,
Already it bears the traces of a pilgrimage:
The impassive eye deciphers in this eloquent spoor
Evidence of struggle and frantic flight,
And here we see some small creature sank.

We cannot foretell what the day will write,
But room is here, yes, room enough is here
For all its recorded heritage
Of blow and falter, blot and tear.
This will be no page to turn with a yawn.

Broken twig and brittle pod will mark their fall,
Soot will sprinkle its ugly pocks,
And cutting across on the diagonal
Will be printed the hesitant tracks
Of some unknown aimless trespasser.

Crack and soilure, seam and scar—
Not one line shall be repealed.
These are the conditions that must obtain
Before pock, trace, print, and blur
Are washed by the sunset stain.

Christmas

Isaiah 53:3

The familiar figures of the crèche,
The familiar props, the familiar stable,
All matter-of-fact, all in the flesh,
As if in a dream, as if in a fable.

The gold and frankincense and myrrh,
The home-made raiment, the vegetable dyes,
The shepherds and wise men in miniature,
The cattle with their knowing eyes.

Mary and Joseph, and the star which glows
With loud Hosannas and good Good-morrows,
The babe wrapped in his swaddling clothes—
Not yet acquainted with grief,
Not yet a man of sorrows.

Signs of the Times

Would you see a sign?—*Yes, we would, we would see a sign.*—
Then look not for famine and plague spot to break forth;
Look not for deluge, earthquake, hail of fire and brimstone,
Nor descent of brute barbarians out of the dark North.
Turn not your eyes upon the heavens for trail of shooting stars;
Seek not the bloody moon that stains the night dew,
Nor marvels like comets, eclipses, zodiacal wars.
Such omens are for the savage, they are not for you.

Here is a sign. A man stacks papers with finical care.
His last look keeps objects in their customary places.
He tries the windows, the door.
He averts his startled eyes from oncoming faces.
He sets down figures in a ledger, the columns are neat.
He crosses each *t*. He does whatever he does in a stipulated way.
He moves a vase one inch to the right and fingers an ornamental
    plate.
That lingering touch holds the shadows at bay.

Here is a sign. Not a book is out of place on his shelf.
Somewhere beyond, on the other side, the enemy is loose;
But on this side he has fettered and confined himself—
Constraints marking the conditions of an uneasy truce.
By what stratagems he has achieved this delicate equipoise!
Yet it will not last. No, the thing will not die when he is dead.
Already, even now, by unwitting gesture and tone of voice,
The sac has been broken, the hidden infection has spread.

So Goes the Report

Out in the vast Pacific, they say,
There is a line which stepped across
Carries you back to yesterday;
And seen through the vapory ectoplasm
The sun's each colored radius
Converging there upon time's prism
Is pulled backward to reunite
In a single shaft of morning light.

There can the swollen leaf be seen
Retract into the infant bud,
Its dark dissolve to tender green;
There the gross and gravid flower
Withdraws into its maidenhood,
The day shrinks back into the hour,
And music's convoluted sound
To its beginning is unwound.

There under her first lover's hand
The woman turns once again the girl,
And man's wisdom weary-brained
Retreats into the child's bright heart.
There skin and flesh glow like the pearl,
There, yes there!—So goes the report.
But here, though our eyes yearn for the East,
Our feet are ever pointed West.

Afternoon of a Faun

Out there in the garden's patched light and shade,
Where fruit tree comes to bear and grapes grow ripe,
Where locust hum muffles a hidden pipe
And all is appetite and escapade,
A glimmer of horn bud and pointed ear
Behind leaf and flower, whose only tense
Is present, and knowing not the dissonance
Of outer and inner, goes unaware

That someone is here, here on the inside,
Peeping out through the bars of the casement,
Sitting in the damp of self-abasement,
Twitching with the capricious cramp of pride,
Straining and heaving, yet unable to cast
The appointed future, the compelling past.

To a Lump of Coal

Ignite and burn!
Wake from the million-year dream
Of jungle steam
And giant fern.

Unlock the sun, burn bright!
Keep off the paralysis
Of ice
And bitter night.

In Praise of Man

Lay out the parts and weigh them in your hand:
Rods and cones, retina, gelatin lens—
The eye! Out of what scanty evidence
Of light-waves it contrives a fantasy land.

Put these together with a certain skill:
Three little bones, a bit of tautened skin.
You have the ear, which makes a bulletin
Out of each sound—to warn, to lure, to thrill.

Yet not content with these marvels, man's heart
Weaves threads from its tangled skein
Of fear and hope into a tapestry
Cunning and rare. And man's sedulous brain
Mixes reverie and thought with deft art
To yield its self-deluding sorcery.

Grisaille with a Spot of Red

Winter, and the sky is a land of gray fiords
Where fogs drift and clouds twist,
All hung over with smoke and mist;
And blown across, three gray rags of birds.

Hill joined to hill by rough gray solders,
Earth is all ash and iron, lead and stone;
Trees are stripped to the brittlest of bone,
And behind and within lurk dim gray hiders.

And there across the gray countryside
Coils a highway, slate on steel:
And over the gray threshold, towards the gray goal,
Flashes an auto, red as blood.

Hope Not Being Hope

hope not being hope
until all ground for hope has
vanished
—MARIANNE MOORE
The Hero

Hope not being a thing of feathers,
Peacock sapphire, bronze, and green,
Toucan yellow, flamingo scarlet,
All flutter, swoop, and color clang:
The thing of feathers is the dream,
Takes wing for Never-Never Land,
Comes to roost in a blasted tree,
A gray bedraggled effigy.

And hope not being jeweled scales,
Iridescent dolphin sparkle,
Chinese dragon flash and flame,
Bright expectation in the hand:
The thing of scales is the wish,
Slips away to the Seven Seas,
Comes to rest on sunless mud,
Light snuffed out, a leaden gaud.

And hope not being a thing of flesh,
Panther velvet, tiger tissue,
Stallion metal, reindeer grace,
Supple sleek seductive woman:
The thing of flesh is self-deception,
Flesh falls in, turns to fat,
And even as we name the shape
Becomes a lewd contorted jape.

Hope not being, not being hope
Until all ground for hope has vanished:
Pluck the feather, scrape the scale,
Strip the flesh down to the frame.
Color, light, and grace extinguished,
No flattering unction on the soul,
Hope is hope when all is gone
But naked sinew, nerve, and bone.

The Child to the Three Wise Men

Christmas 1969
(The first line is an inscription painted by a student, or perhaps a non-student, on the sidewalk leading to Ballantine Hall at Indiana University.)

Do you love the baby Jesus?
Then where you see him in the fields of Zion,
Bring your gold and frankincense and myrrh
To the baby lamb playing with the baby lion.

Do you love the baby Jesus?
Then bring him not the same old faces
Of greed, hypocrisy, and hate,
And public liars in public places.

Do you love the baby Jesus?
How long must he wait for war to cease?
And when at last will you bring as gift
Peace and good will, good will and peace?

The Minor Poet

He comes to you with apologetic smile
At hearing himself called Poet, by the same word,
With Chaucer and Shakespeare, Milton and Pope,
As a starling may with an eagle be called Bird.

And he sidles over in the shadow of Yeats,
Knowing for himself no ladder springs
From the foul rag-and-bone shop of the heart
To where soul claps its hands and sings.

His vein is too thin for Stevens' tropics
Smeared with the gold of the opulent sun;
Nor can he like Hart Crane make
A grail of laughter of an empty ash-can.

He knows Eliot's infirm glory of the positive hour,
And with Frost admires the dauntlessness
Of Man standing alone in a desert
Which has no expression, nothing to express.

But he cannot find the bone-deep word,
His talent, alas, is far too small;
Nor can he call forth the whirling demons
Where mind is Hopkins' cliffs of fall.

Even the scholars intimidate him
With their levels of meaning, their analyses,
Their frames of reference, their mythic myths,
Their personae, and their artistic strategies.

And he is terrified by the critics,
Who get up from their judgment-seats
To use his poem as a trampoline
On which to perform their tumbling feats.

When he looks out at the world about him
Where man commits unbelievable crimes
Against man, with his weak words
How shall he write a fable for our times?

And when the loud aggressive voices shout
War and Hate, Money and Power,
How with this rage shall his poem hold a plea
Whose action is no stronger than a flower?

Yes, he confesses to a bleeding heart,
His intellect quivers at the fingertips;
He sees in each day a parable,
He vaguely senses the Apocalypse.

And he brings you his genteel banalities,
The borrowed line, the echoed phrase,
The rhymes, the grace notes, the filigrees,
The sonnets, ballades, and virelays,
Hoping against hope that someone cares,
That someone somewhere wants his wares.